J B For
O'Shei Tim.
Gerald R. Ford /

PRESIDENTS

GERALD R. FORD

A MyReportLinks.com Book

Tim O'Shei

MyReportLinks.com Books

an imprint of

 Enslow Publishers, Inc. E

Box 398, 40 Industrial Road
Berkeley Heights, NJ 07922
USA

MyReportLinks.com Books, an imprint of Enslow Publishers, Inc. MyReportLinks is a trademark of Enslow Publishers, Inc.

Library of Congress Cataloging-in-Publication Data

O'Shei, Tim.
   / Tim O'Shei.
     p. cm. — (Presidents)
   Summary: A biography of the thirty-eighth president of the United States, who became president upon the resignation of Richard Nixon. Includes Internet links to Web sites, source documents, and photographs related to Gerald Ford.
   Includes bibliographical references (p.) and index.
   ISBN 0-7660-5050-5
   1. Ford, Gerald R., 1913– —Juvenile literature. 2. Presidents—United States—Biography—Juvenile literature. [1. Ford, Gerald R., 1913– 2. Presidents.] I. Title. II. Series.
E866 .O84 2003
973.925'092—dc21

                        2002003420

Printed in the United States of America

10 9 8 7 6 5 4 3 2 1

To Our Readers:

Through the purchase of this book, you and your library gain access to the Report Links that specifically back up this book.

The Publisher will provide access to the Report Links that back up this book and will keep these Report Links up to date on **www.myreportlinks.com** for three years from the book's first publication date.

We have done our best to make sure all Internet addresses in this book were active and appropriate when we went to press. However, the author and the Publisher have no control over, and assume no liability for, the material available on those Internet sites or on other Web sites they may link to.

The usage of the MyReportLinks.com Books Web site is subject to the terms and conditions stated on the Usage Policy Statement on **www.myreportlinks.com**.

In the future, a password may be required to access the Report Links that back up this book. The password is found on the bottom of page 4 of this book.

Any comments or suggestions can be sent by e-mail to comments@myreportlinks.com or to the address on the back cover.

Contents

MyReportLinks.com Books
Great Books, Great Links, Great for Research!

MyReportLinks.com Books present the information you need to learn about your report subject. In addition, they show you where to go on the Internet for more information. The pre-evaluated Report Links that back up this book are kept up to date on **www.myreportlinks.com**. With the purchase of a MyReportLinks.com Books title, you and your library gain access to the Report Links that specifically back up that book. The Report Links save hours of research time and link to dozens—even hundreds—of Web sites, source documents, and photos related to your report topic.

Please see "To Our Readers" on the Copyright page for important information about this book, the MyReportLinks.com Books Web site, and the Report Links that back up this book.

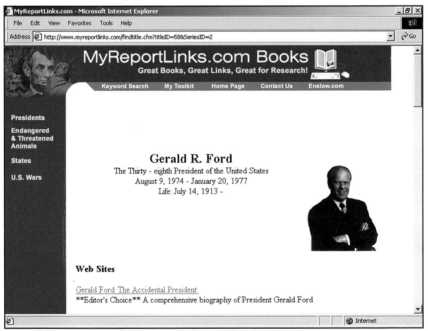

Access:

The Publisher will provide access to the Report Links that back up this book and will try to keep these Report Links up to date on our Web site for three years from the book's first publication date. Please enter **PFO1697** if asked for a password.

Report Links

↗ The Internet sites described below can be accessed at
http://www.myreportlinks.com

*EDITOR'S CHOICE

▶**Gerald Ford: The Accidental President**
At this Web site you will find a comprehensive biography of Gerald
Ford. Learn about his early life, domestic and foreign affairs, the first
lady, and much more.

Link to this Internet site from http://www.myreportlinks.com
*EDITOR'S CHOICE

▶**Gerald R. Ford Library and Museum**
At the Gerald R. Ford Library and Museum you will find historical
documents, photographs, and the biographies of Gerald and Betty
Ford. You can also explore the library's holdings.

Link to this Internet site from http://www.myreportlinks.com
*EDITOR'S CHOICE

▶**The American Presidency: Gerald Ford**
This Web site includes an in-depth biography of Gerald Ford.
Here you will learn about his life, career in congress, vice presidency,
and presidency.

Link to this Internet site from http://www.myreportlinks.com
*EDITOR'S CHOICE

▶***The American President:* Compromise Choices**
This episode of the PBS series, *The American President*, features four
presidents who had to make compromising choices during their
administrations. In this episode you will find a profile about Gerald
Ford and his decision to pardon Nixon.

Link to this Internet site from http://www.myreportlinks.com
*EDITOR'S CHOICE

▶**Presidential Transitions "The Torch is Passed"**
This Web site provides a lesson about Watergate, Gerald Ford,
and the Nixon pardon. Here you will find background information
about Watergate and learn about Ford's transition into the office of
the presidency.

Link to this Internet site from http://www.myreportlinks.com
*EDITOR'S CHOICE

▶**American Presidents: Life Portraits: Gerald Ford**
At this Web site you will find "Life Facts" and "Did you know?" trivia
about Gerald Ford. You will also find a letter written by Ford and
additional Internet resources.

Link to this Internet site from http://www.myreportlinks.com

Report Links

The Internet sites described below can be accessed at
http://www.myreportlinks.com

▶ **The American Presidency: Nelson Rockefeller**
At this Web site you will find the biography of Vice President Nelson
Rockefeller. Here you will learn that Rockefeller served as governor of
New York for four terms.

Link to this Internet site from http://www.myreportlinks.com

▶ **Apollo-Soyuz Test Project**
This Web site tells the story of the Apollo-Soyuz Test Project, the first human
space flight mission managed jointly by two nations. Here you will find a
time line of the mission.

Link to this Internet site from http://www.myreportlinks.com

▶ **Character Above All: Gerald Ford Essay**
At this Web site you will find an essay about Gerald Ford which offers a
look inside his early life and his difficult political decision to pardon
Richard Nixon.

Link to this Internet site from http://www.myreportlinks.com

▶ **Debating our Destiny**
At this PBS Web site, "Debating our Destiny," you can read the transcripts of
the 1976 debate between Jimmy Carter and Gerald Ford. You will also find
the transcripts of interviews with Jimmy Carter, Gerald Ford, and Senator
Bob Dole.

Link to this Internet site from http://www.myreportlinks.com

▶ **The Fall of Saigon 1973–1975**
This site, from the *New York Times*, offers a time line of events between 1973
and 1975 that led to the United States' retreat from Vietnam. Included are
New York Times articles from the time period.

Link to this Internet site from http://www.myreportlinks.com

▶ **The First Eagle Scout, Arthur R. Eldred**
America's Story from America's Library, a Library of Congress Web site tells the
history of Eagle Scouts. Here you will learn about the first Eagle Scout and
other well-known people who have achieved this honor.

Link to this Internet site from http://www.myreportlinks.com

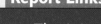
 The Internet sites described below can be accessed at
http://www.myreportlinks.com

▶**Ford, Gerald R.,**
At this Web site you will find a brief introduction to Gerald R. Ford.
Here you will learn about his political career and find a collection of
his speeches including his First Address to Congress and the Nation.

Link to this Internet site from http://www.myreportlinks.com

▶**Ford Lately**
Here you can read the full text of John F. Kennedy, Jr.'s, 1996 interview
with Gerald Ford. By reading this interview you will learn how Ford
felt about his decision to pardon Nixon and other issues he faced in his
vice presidency and presidency.

Link to this Internet site from http://www.myreportlinks.com

▶**Gerald R. Ford**
At this Web site you will find the biography of Gerald Ford, an interesting
fact about him, quotes, a list of important events during his presidency,
and a list of his cabinet members.

Link to this Internet site from http://www.myreportlinks.com

▶**Gerald R. Ford (born 1913)**
At the National Portrait Gallery Web site you can view an oil painting
of Gerald Ford and read a brief biography about him.

Link to this Internet site from http://www.myreportlinks.com

▶**Gerald R. Ford Foundation**
At the Gerald R. Ford Foundation Web site you will find Gerald
Ford's speeches, news of Gerald Ford's current activities, photographs,
information about new exhibits, and more.

Link to this Internet site from http://www.myreportlinks.com

▶**Gerald Rudolph Ford**
This biography of Gerald Ford offers information about his early life,
college, military service, years in congress, and presidency.

Link to this Internet site from http://www.myreportlinks.com

 The Internet sites described below can be accessed at
http://www.myreportlinks.com

▶**Gerald Rudolph Ford**
At this Web site you will find facts and figures on Gerald Ford including
election results, a list of his cabinet members, notable events in his
administration, historic documents, and more.

Link to this Internet site from http://www.myreportlinks.com

▶**Henry A. Kissinger (b. May 27, 1923)**
At this PBS Web site you will find an introduction to Henry Kissinger's life
and learn how in 1973 he and Le Duc Tho were awarded the Nobel Peace
Prize for negotiating an end to the Vietnam War.

Link to this Internet site from http://www.myreportlinks.com

▶**Henry A. Kissinger—Biography**
By navigating through the Nobel e-Museum Web site you will find the
biography of Henry Kissenger, Le Duc Tho, and the 1973 Nobel Prize
presentation speech.

Link to this Internet site from http://www.myreportlinks.com

▶**"I Do Solemnly Swear . . ."**
At this Library of Congress Web site you will find the text of Gerald Ford's
"Remarks Upon Taking the Oath of Office" and an image of him being
sworn in.

Link to this Internet site from http://www.myreportlinks.com

▶**Naval Service of Gerald Ford**
Here you will find information about Gerald Ford's enlistment, service,
combat record, and decoration in the Navy during World War II.

Link to this Internet site from http://www.myreportlinks.com

▶**Objects from the Presidency**
At this site you will find information on all the presidents of the United
States, including Gerald Ford. You can also read a brief description of the era
he lived in and learn about the office of the presidency.

Link to this Internet site from http://www.myreportlinks.com

 The Internet sites described below can be accessed at
http://www.myreportlinks.com

▶**Precious Cargo**
Learn about efforts to save children left homeless by the fall of
Saigon. Gerald Ford allocated two million dollars toward Operation
Babylift which allowed for 2,700 children to be brought over to the
United States.

Link to this Internet site from http://www.myreportlinks.com

▶**President Gerald R. Ford's Proclamation 4311,
Granting a Pardon to Richard Nixon**
At this Web site you will find the speech in which Gerald Ford
pardoned Richard Nixon. There are also links to information about
Watergate, Nixon, and Ford.

Link to this Internet site from http://www.myreportlinks.com

▶**Watergate**
CNN's coverage of Watergate includes Nixon's resignation speech,
Ford's pardon speech, an interview with reporter Bob Woodward, and
excerpts from the Watergate hearings.

Link to this Internet site from http://www.myreportlinks.com

▶**The White House: Elizabeth Bloomer Ford**
The official White House Web site holds the biography of Elizabeth
Bloomer Ford. Here you will learn about her life as a dancer, fashion
model, and first lady.

Link to this Internet site from http://www.myreportlinks.com

▶**The White House: Gerald R. Ford**
The official White House Web site holds the biography of Gerald Ford.
Here you will learn about the challenges he faced during his
administration in domestic and foreign affairs.

Link to this Internet site from http://www.myreportlinks.com

▶**1974: Richard M. Nixon: Thirty-Seventh President of the
United States**
At this PBS Web site you will find a brief overview of Richard Nixon's
presidency and Watergate. You will also find links to additional
information about Watergate.

Link to this Internet site from http://www.myreportlinks.com

Highlights

1913—*July 14:* Born Leslie Lynch King, Jr., in Omaha, Nebraska. His parents, Dorothy Ayer Gardner King and Leslie King, separated sixteen days later.

1914—Moved with his mother to Grand Rapids, Michigan.

1916—*Feb. 1:* Dorothy Gardner King married Gerald Rudolph Ford. The Fords begin calling Leslie, Gerald (or "Jerry") R. Ford, Jr.

1927–1931—Attended South High School in Grand Rapids.

1931–1935—Attended the University of Michigan, where he studied economics and political science. Played football for the Wolverines all four years.

1935–1941—Worked as a boxing and football coach at Yale University. Studied law at Yale full time from 1938 to 1941.

1935—*Dec. 3:* Legally changed his name to Gerald Rudolph Ford.

1941—Opened a law firm in Grand Rapids with fraternity brother Philip Buchen.

1942–1946—Joined the U.S. Navy and served aboard the U.S.S. *Monterey* in World War II. Discharged as a lieutenant commander.

1946–1948—Returned to Grand Rapids and resumed work as a lawyer. Met Elizabeth (Betty) Bloomer Warren.

1948—*Oct. 15:* Married Betty Bloomer Warren. Won election to Congress one month later.

1949—*Jan.:* Began his first term as a Republican U.S. Representative from Michigan's Fifth Congressional District.

1965—Elected House minority leader by his Republican peers.

1973—*Dec. 6:* Sworn in as vice president.

1974—*Aug. 9:* Sworn in as president. Chose Nelson Aldrich Rockefeller as his vice president.

1976—*Nov. 2:* Lost presidential election to Jimmy Carter.

1977—*Jan. 20:* Departed the presidency.

1977–present—In retirement, President Ford gives speeches and interviews, and participates in public service projects. President Ford and Mrs. Ford live in Rancho Mirage, California.

Chapter 1

Assuming the Presidency, 1974

"Are you ready, Mr. Vice President, to assume the presidency in a very short period of time?"[1]

Those were words that Gerald Ford had never wanted to hear. He had hoped to serve as vice president of the United States for the next two years and then retire to a

▲ Seated from left to right are Secretary of State Henry Kissinger, President Richard Nixon, Vice President Gerald Ford, and Chief of Staff Alexander Haig. On August 9, 1974, Nixon became the only president to ever resign from office.

quiet life with his wife, Betty. Unfortunately his boss, President Richard Nixon, was in trouble for covering up a crime. The House of Representatives was poised to impeach Nixon, and the Senate was sure to find the president guilty. The impeachment process focused on the Watergate scandal and could remove Nixon from office. So now, on August 1, 1974, Alexander Haig (the president's top assistant) was posing the question: Was the vice president ready to accept the world's most powerful—and toughest—job?

He was. "If it happens, Al, I am prepared," Gerald Ford replied.[2]

That evening, Ford returned to his home in Alexandria, Virginia and told his wife, Betty, about the conversation with Haig. "My God," she said, "this is going to change our whole life."[3]

Approximately two years earlier, on May 27, 1972, a burglary team hired by members of Nixon's Committee for the Reelection of the President broke into the Democratic National Committee headquarters at the Watergate apartment and office complex in Washington, D.C. The burglars installed telephone bugs and photographed documents. The goal was apparently to produce intelligence on Democratic candidates and on Larry O'Brien, chairman of the Democratic National Committee. On June 17, the burglars once again broke into the Democratic Headquarters to replace a malfunctioning bug. They were discovered and arrested.[4]

Nixon, fearing he might lose the election of 1972 if anyone linked the break-in to his administration, ordered the FBI to halt its investigation of the burglary. He won the election, but revelations about White House staff involvement in the Watergate burglary and its cover-up filled the nightly news.

Now, two years later, Nixon finally released tape recordings of his conversations in the Oval Office. The tapes proved that he was not only aware of a break-in at the Democratic National Committee headquarters, but also that he had taken part in the cover-up.

Vice President Ford stuck to his regular schedule of meetings, ceremonies, and speeches. As much as he tried to make things appear normal, they were not. Nixon's presidency was crumbling. On August 8, 1974, Ford was summoned to the West Wing of the White House for a meeting with the president. President Nixon rose as Ford entered the Oval Office, then he shook his vice president's

▲ Gerald R. Ford was sworn in as the thirty-eighth president of the United States on August 8, 1974.

hand. The two men had become friends twenty-five years earlier, both as young Republican congressmen.

"I have made the decision to resign," Nixon said, and then added, "Jerry, I know you'll do a good job."[5] The two men then talked for an hour about the problems of the country and the world. Nixon did most of the talking; Ford did the listening.

Things were not so calm later on. Nixon was scheduled to announce his resignation on national television at 9:00 P.M. Ford's staff was scrambling to make arrangements for his inaugural ceremony the next day. The event would be held in the East Room of the White House, and 275 guests would be invited. The Chief Justice of the Supreme Court, Warren Burger, was flying back early from a conference in the Netherlands so he could administer the oath of office to Ford.

Richard Milhous Nixon's resignation would go into effect at noon on August 9, 1974. At eleven o'clock, Gerald and Betty Ford accompanied Richard and Pat Nixon across the White House lawn. A helicopter was waiting that would take the outgoing president and his wife away. The two men shook hands and said to each other, "Goodbye, Mr. President."[6]

At noon, with the East Room packed full, Gerald Ford placed his hand on a Bible and swore to uphold the Constitution. Then he turned to the crowd—to the entire world—and began his first speech as the thirty-eighth president of the United States. So many challenges awaited him, so many problems begged to be solved. Americans were counting on Ford to restore honor to the presidency, and he promised to do his job with honesty and grace. "My fellow Americans," he said, "our long national nightmare is over."[7]

Early Life, 1913–1941

Gerald Ford's life was like an adventure. From football stardom to sea battles during World War II, from the floor of the Capitol to the Oval Office, Gerald Ford lived a life as in a movie. Still, perhaps the most dramatic event in his life happened when he was only sixteen days old. Though it would affect his entire future, the young Gerald Ford would not learn about it until he was in his teens.

▶ Leaving Leslie King

The future president was born in Omaha, Nebraska, on July 14, 1913. He was named Leslie Lynch King, Jr. His father, Leslie, Sr., thirty-two, and mother, Dorothy, twenty-one, had been married just eleven months. The marriage had not been a happy one. Leslie had a violent temper and little self-control. The birth of his son did nothing to change that. Shortly after Dorothy returned home from the hospital, Leslie, Sr., threatened his wife and child with a knife.

Ford was born on July 14, 1913. This elementary school portrait was taken in 1923.

Dorothy's parents told her to leave. So did a lawyer. Dorothy knew they were right. Late in July, with her son but sixteen days old, Dorothy slipped out of her house in Omaha. Little Leslie and his mother lived in safety with family until her father was able to set up a home for them in Grand Rapids, Michigan. It was here that Dorothy met a man named Gerald Ford who owned a paint business. The two fell in love and were married when Leslie was just two years old. Dorothy's new husband took the boy as his own son, and they began calling him Gerald (or "Jerry") Ford. Dorothy and Jerry, Sr., would have three sons together.

Jerry along with his half-brothers, Tom, Dick, and James, would learn and follow three rules at home: "Tell the truth, work hard, and don't dare be late for dinner."[1]

▶ Controlling His Temper

Jerry grew up like most boys, playing sports whenever he could. "I went to Madison [Elementary] School," he recalled, "which was an old school. We had a playground in the back that was just plain gravel and dirt, no grass. But it gave us a place where younger kids like myself in those days could congregate after school and play."[2]

During his grade school days, Jerry had a bit of a temper. If he made a mistake at home, he would often blow up in anger. Dorothy quickly put a stop to that. "It was not easy, but my mother was firm and consistent in not tolerating my 'blowing off,' so to speak," Ford remembered. "She knew that a temper of that kind was a bad characteristic that had to be controlled."[3]

It was only around that time that Jerry learned that the man he called Dad was not his birth father. "The truth is, I didn't realize my stepfather was not my real father until I was 10 or 12, or in there someplace," said Ford, whose name was not legally changed until he was an adult. "Even then, it was not a matter of any consequence in our family."[4]

Activities

When he reached South High School, Jerry became a football player right away. The football coach at South noticed the tall, blond ninth-grader and said, "Hey, Whitey, you be the center. Grab the ball."[5] For the next eight years (high school and college), Ford played center for his school's football team. In addition, Ford enjoyed being a Boy Scout. He achieved their highest rank, Eagle Scout, in 1927.

The First Eagle Scout, Arthur R. Eldred - Microsoft Internet Explorer

File   Edit   View   Favorites   Tools   Help

Address http://www.americaslibrary.gov/pages/jb_0821_eaglesco_1_e.html   Go

This poster of Boy Scouts in front of the Capitol in 1941 was used to promote patriotism during World War II

Credit: Rous, John, photographer. "United Nations Fight for Freedom: Boy Scouts in Front of Capitol." Circa July

Internet

▲ Jerry joined the Boy Scouts and achieved the rank of Eagle Scout. When he became vice president in 1973, he would proudly call himself the first "Eagle Scout vice president."

▶ I Am Your Father

A couple of years later, Jerry got a job working at a local hamburger stand called Skougis.' One day, he noticed a man staring at him from across the counter. After several minutes, the man introduced himself as Leslie King, Jerry's father. Mr. King insisted that Jerry leave work early so he could take him to lunch. Jerry did, but found the whole experience upsetting. "That was the first time, as far as I knew, I had met my real father," he said. "The more difficult thing was not going to lunch with him, although that was strained, but to come home that night and tell my mother and stepfather what had transpired. That was very difficult. My mother had such strong anti-feelings against my real father because of his physical and mental abuse of her. She never forgave him, and I don't blame her."[6]

▶ The First Compromise

After graduating from Grand Rapids South High in 1929, Jerry enrolled at the University of Michigan, where he continued playing football and was named best freshman player. In his sophomore and junior years, Ford was a backup center as Michigan had two straight undefeated, national-championship seasons.

In the fall of 1934, Ford became starting center and was named team captain. The Wolverines stumbled, losing their first two games. The third game was against Georgia Tech, but the southern school sent a shocking message the week before the game: If Michigan played Ford's friend Willis Ward—a speedy wide receiver—then Georgia Tech would refuse to take the field. Why? Ward was an African American, and Georgia was segregated back in 1934. "I couldn't believe it," said Ford.[7] In those days, segregation meant separate schools for whites and blacks in some areas of the United States. Officials from both schools worked out an arrangement by which Ward would sit out, and so would a Georgia Tech star. Ford was so angry that his friend had to convince him to play. "Look, the team's having a bad year," Ward told Ford. "We've lost two games already, and we probably won't win anymore. You've got to play Saturday. You owe it to the team."[8]

Often politicians need to compromise, or give into someone else's demands in order to accomplish something good. That is exactly what Ford did during that week. He played in the game that weekend and helped Michigan beat Georgia Tech, 9–2. Years later, as a congressman, vice president, and president, Ford remembered the story of Willis Ward. "It certainly had an impact on my legislative

Jerry Ford was a husky boy who excelled in football. He was offered two National Football League contracts. Here he is shown as the center for the University of Michigan Wolverines.

attitude toward civil rights," Ford said. "I said the Willis Ward situation was unconscionable, and that was only an indication of the tragedy of adverse race relations. So it was a shocker to me."[9]

▶ Choosing the Future

Ford was offered two National Football League contracts: one from the Detroit Lions, the other from the Green Bay Packers. With the opportunity to play pro football only a signature away, Ford turned them down. Instead, he accepted an offer to work at Yale University as the football team's offensive line coach and as the coach of the freshman boxing team. With no previous experience as a boxer, the energetic Ford immediately began taking boxing lessons. He wanted this opportunity. While he coached, Ford could then attend Yale's law school part time and, eventually, full time. "Even though I was tempted to accept either the Lions or Packers offer," Ford said, "I made a judgment that I've never regretted to go to Yale, where I could earn a living and, at the same time, get a legal education."[10]

While still coaching, Ford was a full-time law student from 1938 to 1941. He managed to rank in the top 25 percent of his class and graduate with offers to work for law firms in New York and Philadelphia. He chose instead to return home to Grand Rapids, Michigan, to open a law firm with college friend Philip A. Buchen. (Buchen would later serve as Counsel to the President during Ford's administration.) Both men worked hard and put in long hours building their firm. Yet World War II was about to pull Gerald Ford away to a new place—a place where he would fight for freedom.

Chapter 3

Young Adulthood, 1941–1949

Driving home from his office on the night of Sunday, December 7, 1941, Ford turned on the radio. Right away, he heard the news: Japanese planes had attacked a United States naval base in Pearl Harbor, Hawaii. The next day, Ford signed up for the Navy. After a stint at the Naval Academy in Maryland, his first job was as a physical fitness instructor at a base in North Carolina. Ford was not

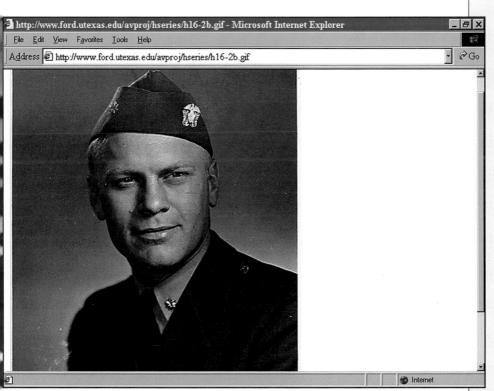

http://www.ford.utexas.edu/avproj/hseries/h16-2b.gif - Microsoft Internet Explorer

File   Edit   View   Favorites   Tools   Help

Address http://www.ford.utexas.edu/avproj/hseries/h16-2b.gif   Go

Internet

▲ Gerald Ford signed up for the navy the day after the attack on Pearl Harbor. In 1946, he was discharged as a lieutenant commander.

happy with that; he wanted to be part of the action. "There was a war going on," he wrote in his autobiography. "I wanted desperately to be a part of it."[1]

After sending several letters asking to be assigned to a ship, Ford was ordered to report to the U.S.S. *Monterey* in the spring of 1943. He became athletic director and a gunnery officer, responsible for firing an antiaircraft gun. The *Monterey* headed to the South Pacific, where Ford took part in ten battles over the next two years. The *Monterey* "took part in major operations in the South Pacific, including Truk, Saipan, and the Phillipines."[2] His closest brush with death overseas, however, was not during a battle. In the South Pacific, typhoons would sometimes strike across the waters. In one vicious storm, Ford was almost knocked overboard. He clung only to a railing to save his life. "I fell halfway in and halfway out," he told an interviewer years later. "If I had gone another foot, I'd have gone over the side."[3]

Ford spent the final part of his military duty working out of the Naval Reserve Training Command in Glenview, Illinois. Surprisingly, that job nearly killed him, too. In the fall of 1945, he was on a flight to his old base in Chapel Hill. During the landing approach, the pilot made an error and crashed the plane. Ford and his fellow passengers struggled out of the plane seconds before it exploded.

▶ A Man Discharged—and Changed

Lieutenant Commander Ford was discharged from the Navy in February 1946. He returned to Grand Rapids, where he joined the law firm of Butterfield, Keeney, and Amberg. Back in Grand Rapids, Gerald Ford was active in his community. He poured all his energy into his job and, whenever he could squeeze some extra time, volunteered to help out with community activities, too. He liked people and he liked to be involved.

▶ He Also Liked a Lady

In 1947, Gerald Ford was thirty-four years old and single. His younger half-brothers were raising families; his mother and stepfather were gently pushing him to date. Friends helped Ford set up a date with a girl he remembered from high school, Betty Bloomer, who was getting a divorce. Betty, a department store fashion coordinator and former dancer, was also busy with her job. Yet they saw each other as much as they could and quickly fell in love. On an evening in February 1948, Gerald told Betty, "I'd like to

http://www.ford.utexas.edu/avproj/hseries/h13-1b.gif - Microsoft Internet Explorer

File   Edit   View   Favorites   Tools   Help

Address   http://www.ford.utexas.edu/avproj/hseries/h13-1b.gif   Go

Done   Internet

▲ Gerald Ford and Betty Bloomer were married on October 15, 1948.

marry you." Then he added, "But we can't get married until next fall, and I can't tell you why."[4]

The Run for Office

Betty said yes, and it did not take long for her to learn of Ford's surprise reason for an autumn wedding. He was going to run for Congress! The local Republican who held the seat, Bartel Jonkman, believed the United States should stay out of disputes in other parts of the world. Ford came back from World War II believing the opposite.[5] He thought America should help its European friends. He decided to run against Jonkman for the nomination for the Republican seat. Most people considered Ford a long shot—Jonkman was well-known and influential in Washington. Yet Ford campaigned daily through the summer and fall, working only one hour each day in the law office. He was nearly late for the wedding on October 15, 1948, because he had been campaigning all morning. Betty understood, and the hard work paid off. Ford won the primary and then took 61 percent of the vote in the general election. He was off to Congress.

Chapter 4

Congress, 1949–1973

Gerald Ford quickly gained power in Washington. Early in his first term, he was appointed to the House Appropriations Committee. This powerful group determines how budget money is spent across the government. Grabbing a spot on that committee helped Ford's rise to prominence. In 1951, he became the ranking minority

▲ Gerald Ford and his wife, Betty, are pictured here with their three sons. Their daughter, Susan, was born in 1957.

member on the Defense Appropriations Subcommittee. Budgeting and military matters soon became his specialties.

Early in his career as the representative from Michigan's Fifth District, Ford made the decision to spend most of his working time in Washington. Ford knew his staff could attend to the needs of his Michigan constituents. Yet only he could debate on the floor of the House and build a network of contacts inside the Capitol building. Choosing to focus his energies in Washington was one of the decisions that eventually allowed Ford to become House minority leader, then vice president, and eventually president. He got to know every powerful person in Washington, including a congressman from California named Richard Nixon. In 1949, they became friends in the House, and their relationship continued, as Nixon became a senator and then vice president to Dwight Eisenhower.

▶ A Good Guy

Gerald and Betty Ford started their family in Washington. In 1950, Michael was born, followed by John in 1952, and Steven in 1956. Their only daughter, Susan, was born in 1957. As his family grew in the nation's capital, so did Ford's influence. Even his political opponents admitted he was hardworking, fair, and honest.

One of Ford's earliest famous friends was a Democratic congressman from Massachusetts named John F. Kennedy. Jack, as his friends called him, would be elected president in 1960. "His office and my office were right across the hall from each other," Ford says. "So I saw him virtually every day and established a very good personal friendship before he went to the Senate and before he became president."[1]

Ford also developed a relationship with the president at the time, Harry Truman. Ford supported Truman's Marshall

Plan for rebuilding European countries after World War II. Ford supported other foreign policy decisions as well, such as Truman's use of United States troops in Korea.

In 1952, Ford worked hard to help elect the Republican president, Dwight Eisenhower. Throughout the 1950s, Ford's reputation as a fair and honest team player became stronger. His loyalty shone, too, when he defended Vice President Nixon against critics who wanted him off the Eisenhower reelection ticket in 1956.

The Warren Commission

By the early 1960s, Ford was recognized as a leader in Republican congressional politics. After President Kennedy's assassination in 1963, President Lyndon

▲ Congressman Ford makes a campaign stop at a farm in Kent County, Michigan, in 1948.

Johnson appointed Ford to serve on the Warren Commission. The Commission investigated the shooting and determined that a single assassin, Lee Harvey Oswald, had killed the president. Ford found the hearings difficult. "It was an emotional experience to listen to the testimony of people who had been at the point of the assassination," he said. "After all, I had this long-standing personal friendship with President Kennedy, and to sit there in the commission hearing and seeing the gory details about the shots from the schoolbook depository, to see the photographs and everything involved in the assassination, caused a very emotional reaction."[2] Ford co-authored, with John R. Stiles, a book about the investigation entitled *Portrait of the Assassin.*

▶ Leader of the Minority

Ford's long-term goal was to become Speaker of the House. For that to happen, there would have to be more Republicans elected to the House of Representatives than Democrats. In the meantime, the highest post Ford could achieve would be House minority leader. In January 1965, he was elected to that post by his Republican peers in the House.

Over the following four years, Ford was one of President Johnson's loudest critics. Ford especially disagreed with Johnson's handling of the Vietnam War. He wanted the president to either launch a full-blown attack or pull out of Vietnam. "Why are we pulling our best punches in Vietnam?" he asked in a 1967 speech on the floor of the House. "Is there no end, no other answer, except more men, more men, more men?"[3]

Johnson attacked Ford, too. In one speech, he said that Ford "spent too much time playing football without a helmet."[4] Though the two were arch political enemies, Johnson and Ford respected each other as people. "We enjoyed each other's company," Ford said. "He was very critical of me and I would reciprocate with him in the political arena. But we had a good personal relationship."[5]

The Final Stretch on Capitol Hill

Johnson decided not to run for reelection in 1968, and Richard Nixon won the presidency over Democrat Hubert Humphrey. Not surprisingly, Ford was a strong Nixon supporter; both men were Republicans.

▲ In 1975, after the United States had pulled out of Vietnam, President Gerald Ford allocated $2 million to airlift 2,700 Vietnamese orphans to the United States.

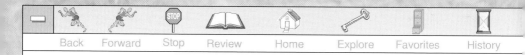
By early 1973, the Republicans had not succeeded in taking the majority in Congress. Ford realized that he was not going to become Speaker of the House. He was traveling over two hundred nights per year, making speeches, and raising campaign funds around the country. Of those times Ford reflected, "I was gone more than I wanted to be, but I had a job to do. I always reserved two to three weeks where we had a family vacation. . . . That helped to make up for the other days that I was gone extensively."[6] Actually, he was beginning to wonder if perhaps he should leave politics and resume a private career as a lawyer.[7]

▶ A New Job Offer

On Friday morning, October 12, 1973, Ford was called to the White House. He thought he was being called to discuss some legislation in Congress.

Two days earlier, Vice President Spiro Agnew had resigned. Agnew, under investigation at the time, was later convicted of income tax evasion. President Nixon needed a new vice president. After considering three other people, Nixon decided upon Gerald Ford as his top choice. Ford told Nixon that he had promised Betty he would retire in January 1977. Since that was exactly when Nixon's second term would end, the offer worked out perfectly. Ford accepted Nixon's proposal to become vice president of the United States.

▶ A Slower Pace

Though the vice presidency is the number two job in the government, the actual powers of the position are few. Vice presidents do not make policy; presidents do. Vice presidents do not vote on laws unless the Senate is tied, 50–50. Mainly, vice presidents do whatever they can to support the president—which was precisely Ford's role. With his clean reputation and many friends in Congress, Ford would be able to push the policies and views of his more controversial boss. After an FBI background check and confirmation hearings in Congress, during which Ford promised he would not run for president in 1976, the

▲ Congressman Ford introduces Nixon during Nixon's campaign for president in 1968.

House and Senate approved Ford's appointment.[8] On December 6, 1973, Ford became the first person to be appointed vice president under the Twenty-fifth Amendment to the Constitution.

During the eight months he spent as vice president, Ford traveled the country trying to gain support for the Nixon White House. One of his roles was to defend the president in the Watergate investigation. Nixon had taped conversations in the Oval Office, and now Watergate investigators wanted the tapes.

Ford urged Nixon to turn over the tapes. When Nixon did hand over the recordings, eighteen minutes were missing from one of the tapes. Nixon chose to announce the release of the edited tapes directly to the people in a television address. He hoped to win support from the American people by appealing to their sense of fairness. Sadly, he had failed to grasp the depth of his fellow Americans' outrage over the Watergate scandal and its cover-up, which had been played out daily in the media for nearly a year.[9]

Finally, facing impeachment, Nixon resigned on August 9, 1974. Gerald R. Ford became the first and only chief executive to take the oath of office without having been elected to either the vice presidency or the presidency.

In the White House, 1974–1977

The American people warmly accepted Gerald Ford as their new president. He seemed peaceful, calm, and honest—three refreshing qualities for a leader.

As he began work in the White House, Ford asked whether the tape recording systems that Nixon and Johnson had used were still around. Told that some were, he recalled, "I ordered them to be dismantled. I didn't

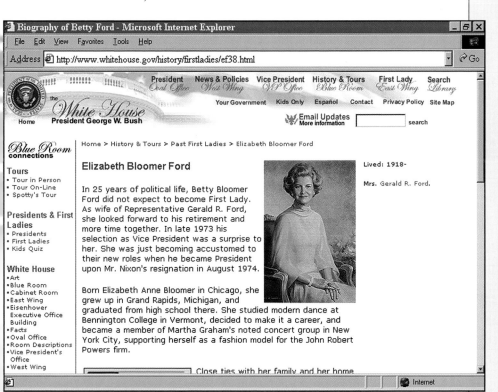

Biography of Betty Ford - Microsoft Internet Explorer

File   Edit   View   Favorites   Tools   Help

Address http://www.whitehouse.gov/history/firstladies/ef38.html   Go

President   News & Policies   Vice President   History & Tours   First Lady   Search
Oval Office   West Wing   VP Office   Blue Room   East Wing   Library

the White House   Your Government   Kids Only   Español   Contact   Privacy Policy   Site Map

Home   President George W. Bush   Email Updates   More information   search

Blue Room connections

Tours
• Tour in Person
• Tour On-Line
• Spotty's Tour

Presidents & First Ladies
• Presidents
• First Ladies
• Kids Quiz

White House
• Art
• Blue Room
• Cabinet Room
• East Wing
• Eisenhower Executive Office Building
• Facts
• Oval Office
• Room Descriptions
• Vice President's Office
• West Wing

Home > History & Tours > Past First Ladies > Elizabeth Bloomer Ford

Elizabeth Bloomer Ford

Lived: 1918-

Mrs. Gerald R. Ford.

In 25 years of political life, Betty Bloomer Ford did not expect to become First Lady. As wife of Representative Gerald R. Ford, she looked forward to his retirement and more time together. In late 1973 his selection as Vice President was a surprise to her. She was just becoming accustomed to their new roles when he became President upon Mr. Nixon's resignation in August 1974.

Born Elizabeth Anne Bloomer in Chicago, she grew up in Grand Rapids, Michigan, and graduated from high school there. She studied modern dance at Bennington College in Vermont, decided to make it a career, and became a member of Martha Graham's noted concert group in New York City, supporting herself as a fashion model for the John Robert Powers firm.

Close ties with her family and her home

Internet

▲ Betty Ford was an advocate for women's rights and supported the Equal Rights Amendment.

want any taping of conversations as had been done during the Nixon and Johnson era."[1]

On August 20, 1974, Ford announced his appointment of former New York governor Nelson A. Rockefeller as vice president. Four months later, after an extensive investigation, Congress approved Rockefeller's appointment.

Ford expected his staff members to be team players. He hated arguing and jealousy and put a stop to it whenever he sensed his staff was wasting time. He did not want his White House to be an imposing picture of power; he wanted it to be a helpful symbol of power. "We didn't want an imperial White House," he said. "We wanted a down-to-earth White House. The minute my staff would take on the imperial White House attitude, boy, I cracked down on them."[2]

▶ At Home in the White House

Gerald Ford had never wanted to be president. Now that he was, he wanted to act and be treated like a normal person as much as possible. Unlike many past presidents, Ford did not like the fancy parts of his job. People who used to call him Jerry now called him "Mr. President," though, as he recalls, "I didn't prompt people to call me that."[3] Ford also ordered the Marine Band to play the University of Michigan fight song instead of "Hail to the Chief" when he entered a room for a ceremony.

Of the four Ford children, only Susan lived in the White House full time. Mike was studying to be a minister, Jack was attending college in Utah; and Steve worked on a cattle ranch in Montana. Susan, who was only seventeen when her family moved into the White House, was able to hold her high school prom in the mansion and enjoyed a huge birthday bash there, too. On the downside, Susan also had to deal with all sorts of attention from the media. "I was criticized," she said, "for everything from wearing blue jeans to dating [her older boyfriend] Brian."[4]

First Lady Betty Ford was an outspoken supporter of women's rights. She encouraged her husband to appoint women to important jobs. She supported the Equal Rights Amendment and the right to have an abortion. To encourage awareness and help other women, Mrs. Ford spoke about her own experience with breast cancer.

The Pardon

At the start of their term, most presidents enjoy a "honeymoon" period in which their popularity soars. Ford had that, but it did not last long—a brief thirty days.

The biggest question facing Ford early in his presidency was whether he would pardon Nixon. The president of the United States has the power to pardon, or excuse, a person from serving punishment for a crime. It was likely that Nixon would be brought to trial for the Watergate affair, and Ford did not want the scandal to be prolonged.

President Gerald Ford announced his pardon of Richard Nixon from the Oval Office on September 8, 1974.

▲ *This photograph captures the moments just following an attempt to assassinate Gerald Ford on September 5, 1975. Lynette Fromme was convicted of attempted assassination and sentenced to life imprisonment.*

He worried that watching a former president stand trial would further divide American opinion, and he wanted to bring people together. So after a few weeks of consulting his staff, Ford made a short announcement in the Oval Office on a Sunday morning in September: He was granting a "full, free, and absolute pardon."[5]

Ford had hoped his decision would help bring peace to the nation. It did not. It actually sparked an avalanche of criticism. Some people were unhappy that Nixon was pardoned before even being indicted for a crime. Others thought he should have to stand trial, just as any normal citizen would. Still others wondered whether Ford had made a deal as vice president. They wondered if the plan was that if Nixon resigned and Ford became president, Ford would then pardon Nixon. Ford has always denied that a deal was made. He testified before Congress, saying, "There was no deal. Period. Under no circumstances."[6]

Many of the people who worked for Ford were unhappy with his pardon decision. His press secretary, Jerald terHorst, quit in protest. Ford has always stuck by his decision and has said that he wished he had pardoned Nixon even earlier. "I have to say that most of my staff disagreed with me over the pardon," Ford said. "But I was absolutely convinced that it was the right thing to do."[7]

▶ A Decision Maker

When he had a big decision to make, Ford listened long and hard to people's opinions. He mulled over his own

▲ In 1974, President Gerald Ford and General Secretary Leonid Brezhnev met in Vladivostok to sign the Vladivostok Accord. This established the framework for future discussions between the United States and the Soviet Union on controlling nuclear weapons.

thoughts, made a decision, and then moved on. Shortly after pardoning Nixon in September 1974, Ford offered a clemency program to people who had evaded the Vietnam War draft. He gave the thousands of draft evaders the chance to clear their record by swearing allegiance to the United States and performing two years of community service. Many veterans' groups felt this punishment was not stiff enough. Though the United States had pulled out of Vietnam during Nixon's era, the war still raged overseas. The Communist forces won, uniting North and South Vietnam into a single country in July 1976.

Under Ford the United States began to slowly ease the tensions of the Cold War. With thirty-four other countries, the United States signed the Helsinki Agreement in 1975, which helped to improve communications between Communist and democratic countries.

Ford's nerves were tested on May 12, 1975, when Cambodia's Khmer Rouge forces seized an American ship called the S.S. *Mayaguez.* After trying to resolve the problem peacefully, Ford ordered a strike by the U.S. Air Force, U.S. Navy, and U.S. Marines to save the thirty-nine-member crew. Tragically, forty-one American lives were lost in the effort, but Congress and the public supported Ford's aggressive move.

Back at home, Ford favored fiscal conservatism, meaning he did not like to see the government spend huge amounts of money on programs. With the American economy in bad shape, he tried to cut the federal budget. The United States was stuck in the worst recession since the Great Depression of the 1930s. Despite his efforts, Ford was unable to pull the country out of it. With the Democrats running Congress, many of his policy ideas were quickly voted down.[8]

▲ *In September 1976, a presidential debate was held between Gerald Ford, right, and Jimmy Carter, left, in Philadelphia.*

▶ Leaving Washington

Ford found he enjoyed being president. He liked it so much that he wanted to continue to serve beyond 1977, which is when he had promised his wife he would retire. Ford narrowly beat California governor Ronald Reagan for the Republican nomination.

In the general election, Ford faced former Georgia governor Jimmy Carter, a little-known Democrat. Early in the campaign, with voters upset over his pardon of Nixon and the poor economy, Ford was more than thirty points behind Carter in the polls. Then, as they campaigned and debated, the race between Ford and Carter became too close to call. On Election Day, November 2, 1976, Carter won, his 50 percent of the vote beating Ford's 48 percent. Though the two men ran a bitter race, Carter acknowledged Ford's accomplishments after he took the oath of office in January 1977. "For myself and for our nation," Carter said, "I want to thank my predecessor for all he has done to heal our land."[9]

Chapter 6 ▶

After the White House, 1977–Present

The Fords said their good-byes to Washington following President Carter's inauguration ceremony, when they boarded a helicopter that would take them to Andrews Air Force Base. At the former president's request, the pilot circled around the dome of the Capitol building. As the helicopter hovered over the place he had served twenty-five years as a congressman, Ford said, "That's my real home."[1] Today, the Gerald R. Ford House of Representatives Office Building pays tribute to those years of service.

The Fords retired to Rancho Mirage, California, where both kept busy. President Ford, who started golfing as a teenager, continued to play the game. He traveled regularly, appearing in charity golf tournaments to help raise money. He also made speeches around the country, and worked as a consultant for several corporations.

After a well-publicized battle and recovery from alcohol and substance addiction in 1978, Mrs. Ford started developing plans for a treatment center. The Betty Ford Center for Drug and Alcohol Rehabilitation opened in Rancho Mirage in 1982.

▶ An Unlikely Friend

In the years immediately following Ford's defeat, he and President Carter did not get along. They had politically opposite philosophies and had fought a close, bitter battle for the White House. In 1981, they found themselves together, along with Richard Nixon, flying on a plane overseas. They were all headed to the Middle East for the funeral of Egyptian president Anwar Sadat. With time to talk, Ford and Carter found that they shared many beliefs about foreign policy. On domestic policy, they were quite divided. What is more, the two former presidents found that they liked each other. In the years since, they have become close friends. "We're good personal friends," Ford said, "and we also have worked together on a number of public interest policies."[2]

▲ Part of the president's job is to entertain other government figures. Here, Ford is shown dancing with Queen Elizabeth II of England during a state dinner in honor of the British Monarch.

IPL POTUS -- Gerald R. Ford Image Gallery - Microsoft Internet Explorer

File Edit View Favorites Tools Help

Address http://www.ipl.org/ref/POTUS/grford/sadat.html   Go

Gerald R. Ford Image Gallery

President Ford meeting with Egyptian President Anwar Sadat in Salzburg, Austria. June 2, 1975.

Internet

▲ *President Gerald Ford met with Egyptian President Anwar Sadat in 1975 to settle a territorial dispute. Both Ford and Carter attended Sadat's funeral in 1981, sparking a lasting friendship between the two former leaders.*

At the end of 1998, as President Bill Clinton was facing impeachment and possible removal from office, Presidents Ford and Carter wrote an editorial for the *New York Times.* They favored a bipartisan resolution of censure by the Senate. Accordingly, President Clinton would have to acknowledge his wrongdoing and accept the rebuke. Again, after the contentious election of George W. Bush over Al Gore in November 2000, Ford and Carter co-chaired a committee that studied election reform. "The issue," said Ford, "is what can we do to improve the election process and procedures in the future?"[3]

▶ **The Legacy of Gerald Ford**

Ford is largely remembered as the only man to ascend to both the vice presidency and presidency of the United States without ever getting elected. Along with that distinction, people also know him as the president who pardoned Richard Nixon. Many historians feel that the pardon—which was unpopular at the time—caused his loss to Carter. In the years since, however, many people have come to believe that Ford made the proper decision. In May 2001, he received the John F. Kennedy Profile In Courage Award for making a "decision of conscience."[4]

As the millennium turned, President Ford remained visible to the public. He still gives occasional interviews and keeps up on politics. On August 1, 2000, he was honored at the Republican National Convention in Philadelphia. On the same night he was recognized, President Ford suffered a stroke and was hospitalized for most of the next week. He made a full recovery, however, and was able to watch the campaign proceedings over the next few months. When Governor George W. Bush of Texas won the presidency, Ford saw two of his former White House aides assume positions in the new administration: Donald H. Rumsfeld, Ford's secretary of defense, fills the same position for Bush. Dick Cheney, who at one time was Ford's chief of staff, is Bush's vice president.

Like the rest of America, President Ford witnessed the terrorist attacks of September 11, 2001. Perhaps he felt the same as he did nearly sixty years earlier, when he heard about the bombing of Pearl Harbor. In December 1941, he responded by joining the navy. At age eighty-eight, he used his words—powerful tools for former presidents. Ford spoke of patriotism, unity, and greatness:

President Ford and Ronald Reagan shake hands to show Republican solidarity at the Republican National Convention on August 19, 1976. In August 2000, Ford was honored at the Republican National Convention held in Philadelphia.

Like every American, I take heart from President Bush's resolute leadership. Today there are no partisans in Washington, only patriots. No doubt the weeks ahead will pose fresh tests of our national unity. As a member of the so-called Greatest Generation, I have no doubt that the current generation of Americans will demonstrate its own character and courage—even as the heroic people of New York have reminded us yet again that theirs is the greatest city on Earth.[5]

Chapter Notes

Chapter 1. Assuming the Presidency, 1974

1. Bob Woodward, *Shadow* (New York: Simon & Schuster, 1999), p. 6.

2. Gerald R. Ford, *A Time To Heal: The Autobiography of Gerald R. Ford* (New York: Harper & Row, 1979), p. 3.

3. Ibid.

4. Richard Reeves, *President Nixon: Alone in the White House* (New York: Simon & Schuster, 2001), p. 499.

5. Ford, p. 28.

6. Betty Ford, *The Times of My Life* (New York: Harper & Row, 1978), p. 3.

7. Woodward, p. 14.

Chapter 2. Early Life, 1913–1941

1. Bonnie Angelo, *First Mothers: The Women Who Shaped the Presidents* (New York: William Morrow, 2000), p. 236.

2. Personal interview with former President Gerald Ford, February 1, 2001.

3. Ibid.

4. Ibid.

5. Tim O'Shei, "From One Battlefield to Another," *Football Digest*, Dec. 1999, p. 48.

6. Personal interview with former President Gerald Ford, February, 1, 2001.

7. O'Shei, p. 46.

8. Ibid.

9. Ibid., p. 47.

10. Ibid., p. 50.

Chapter 3. Young Adulthood, 1941–1948

1. Gerald R. Ford, *A Time to Heal: The Autobiography of Gerald R. Ford* (New York: Harper & Row, 1979), p. 58.

2. "Gerald R. Ford Biography," n.d., <http://www.ford.utexas.edu/grf/fordbiop.htm> (May 23, 2002).

3. John Hersey, *The President: A Minute-by-Minute Account of a Week in the Life of Gerald Ford* (New York: Knopf, 1975), p. 93.

4. Ford, p. 65.

5. Philip B. Kunhardt, Jr., Philip B. Kunhardt III, Peter W. Kunhardt, *The American President* (New York: Riverhead Books/Penguin Putnam, 1999), p. 79.

Chapter 4. Congress, 1949–1973

1. Personal interview with former President Gerald Ford, February 1, 2001.

2. Ibid.

3. William A. DeGregorio, *The Complete Book of U.S. Presidents* (New York: Dembner Books, 1984), pp. 608–609.

4. Ibid., p. 614.

5. Personal interview with former President Gerald Ford, February 1, 2001.

6. Ibid.

7. David C. Whitney and Robin Vaughn Whitney, *The American Presidents*, 7th edition (New York: Prentice Hall Press, 1990), p. 372.

8. Diana Dixon Healy, *America's Vice-Presidents* (New York: Antheneum, 1984), p. 216.

9. Richard Nixon, *Presidential Politics*, n.d., <http://www.pbs.org.wgbh/amex/presidents/frames/featured/nixon/nixonpp.html> (May 23, 2002).

Chapter 5. In the White House, 1974–1977

1. Personal interview with former President Gerald Ford, February 1, 2001.

2. Ibid.

3. Ibid.

4. Susan Edwards, *White House Kids* (New York: Avon Books, 1999), p. 117.

5. George Sullivan, *Mr. President: A Book of U.S. Presidents* (New York: Scholastic, 2001), p. 147.

6. James Cannon, *Character Above All: Gerald Ford*, n.d., <http://www.pbs.org/newshour/character/essays/ford.html> (July 21, 2001).

7. Philip B. Kunhardt, Jr., Philip B. Kunhardt III, Peter W. Kunhardt, *The American President* (New York: Riverhead Books/Penguin Putnam, 1999), p. 81.

8. "President Ford's Leadership," n.d., <http://www.ford.utexas.edu/library/document/factbook/accompli.htm> (June 7, 2002).

9. William A. DeGregorio, *The Complete Book of U.S. Presidents* (New York: Dembner Books, 1984), p. 614.

Chapter 6. After the White House, 1977–Present

1. Gerald R. Ford, *A Time to Heal: The Autobiography of Gerald R. Ford* (New York: Harper & Row, 1979), p. 442.

2. Personal interview with former President Gerald Ford, February 1, 2001.

3. Ibid.

4. "President Gerald Ford Named Recipient of 2001 John F. Kennedy Profile in Courage Award," *John Fitzgerald Kennedy Library*, April 28, 2001, <http://www.jfklibrary.org/pr_pica2001_announce.html> (September 11, 2002).

5. Gerald Ford, Official Statement from September 12, 2001.

Angelo, Bonnie. *First Mothers: The Women Who Shaped the Presidents*. New York: William Morrow, 2000.

Boller, Paul F., Jr., *Presidential Anecdotes*. New York: Oxford University Press, 1996.

Edwards, Susan. *White House Kids*. New York: Avon Books, 1999.

Ford, Betty. *The Times of My Life*. New York: Harper & Row, 1978.

Ford, Gerald R. *A Time to Heal: The Autobiography of Gerald R. Ford*. New York: Harper & Row, 1979.

Fremon, David K. *The Watergate Scandal in American History*. Berkeley Heights, N.J.: Enslow Publishers, Inc., 1998.

Gormley, Beatrice. *First Ladies: Women Who Called the White House Home*. New York: Scholastic, 1997.

Hersey, John. *The President: A Minute-by-Minute Account of a Week in the Life of Gerald Ford*. New York: Knopf, 1975.

Krull, Kathleen. *Lives of the Presidents*. New York: Harcourt Brace, 1998.

Kunhardt, Philip B. Jr., et. al. *The American President*. New York: Riverhead Books/Penguin Putnam, 1999.

Morris, Juddi. *At Home with the Presidents*. New York: John Wiley & Sons, Inc., 1999.

Sullivan, George. *Mr. President: A Book of U.S. Presidents*. New York: Scholastic, 2001.